PICTURE LIBRARY

SEALS AND WALRUSES

PICTURE LIBRARY

SEALS AND WALRUSES

Norman Barrett

Franklin Watts

New York   London   Sydney   Toronto

© 1991 Franklin Watts

Franklin Watts Inc
387 Park Avenue South
New York, N.Y. 10016

Library of Congress Cataloging-in-Publication Data

Barrett, Norman S.
    Seals and walruses/Norman Barrett.
        p. cm. — (Picture library)
    Summary: Depicts the habitat, feeding habits, and life cycle of
seals and walruses.
    ISBN 0-531-14115-2
    1. Seals (Animals)—Juvenile literature. 2. Walruses—Juvenile
literature. [1. Seals (Animals) 2. Walruses.] I. Title.
II. Series.
QL737.P64B38 1991
599.74'5—dc20

90-32150
CIP AC

Printed in the United Kingdom

Designed by
Barrett and Weintroub

Research by
Deborah Spring

Photographs by
Survival Anglia
N.S. Barrett

Illustration by
Rhoda and Robert Burns

Technical Consultant
Michael Chinery

Contents

Introduction

Seals and walruses are mammals that live in the sea and have their young on land. They have streamlined bodies, shaped like torpedoes. Their powerful flippers make them excellent swimmers.

There are two main kinds of seals: true seals and eared seals. With walruses, they make up a group of the animal kingdom called pinnipeds.

△ A two-week-old baby seal, or pup. Female seals usually have just one pup at a time. Most pups are normally born with a coat of fine, soft fur.

Most seals live in the cool waters of the polar regions. They breed on ice and rocky shores.

There are 19 different species (kinds) of true seals. They include the common, elephant and leopard seals.

The 14 species of eared seals are better known as fur seals and sea lions.

The walrus is the only member of its family. Walruses are found only in Arctic seas.

△ A walrus is easily recognized because of its long, white tusks. Walruses have a thick, creased skin covered with coarse hair. Adult males have very little hair.

Looking at seals and walruses

There are two kinds of seals: true seals and eared seals. True seals can spend more time underwater, and are more streamlined and flexible. They swim using side-to-side movements of the rear part of the body. Eared seals move more easily on land, using their strong front flippers to raise their bodies. Both have dense fur and thick layers of blubber (fat) to conserve their body heat.

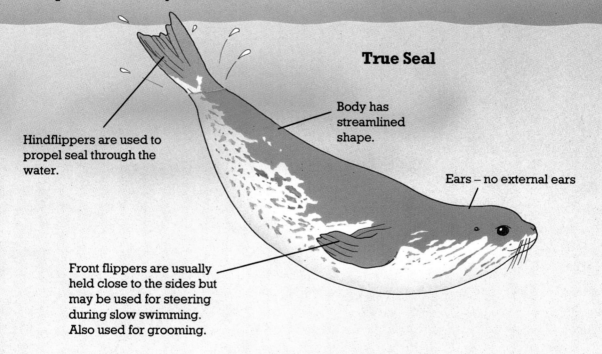

True Seal

Hindflippers are used to propel seal through the water.

Body has streamlined shape.

Ears – no external ears

Front flippers are usually held close to the sides but may be used for steering during slow swimming. Also used for grooming.

Shapes and sizes of seals and walruses

(average length of males – females are always much smaller)

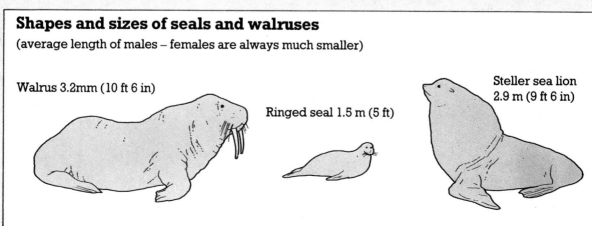

Walrus 3.2mm (10 ft 6 in)

Ringed seal 1.5 m (5 ft)

Steller sea lion 2.9 m (9 ft 6 in)

Flippers

The sea lion's hind flipper (1) has no claws, only slight nodules, set back from the end of the flipper, which has elongated "toes." Northern true seals (2) have distinct claws, and southern true seals (3) have webs of tough skin between their "toes," making the hind flipper an effective paddle.

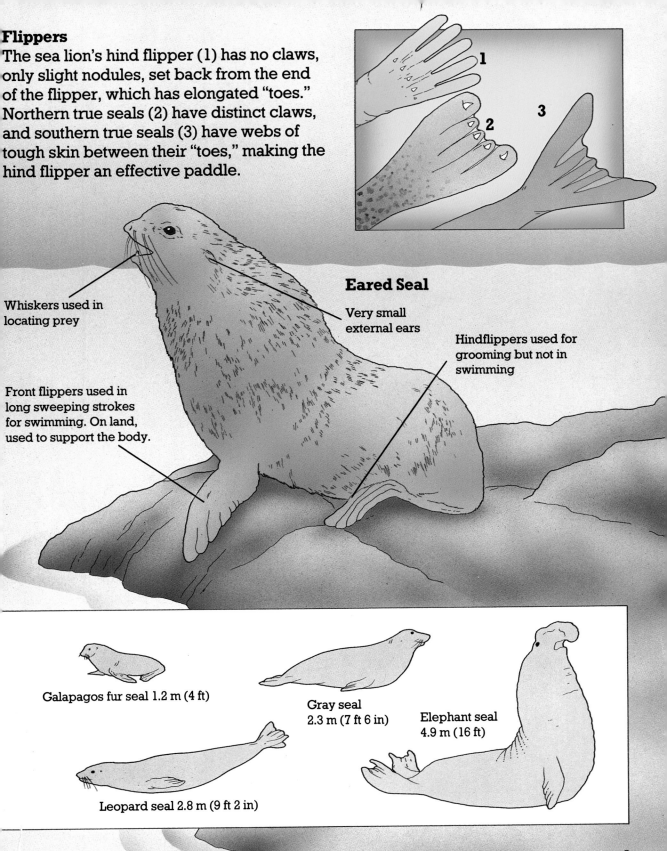

Eared Seal

Whiskers used in locating prey

Very small external ears

Hindflippers used for grooming but not in swimming

Front flippers used in long sweeping strokes for swimming. On land, used to support the body.

Galapagos fur seal 1.2 m (4 ft)

Gray seal 2.3 m (7 ft 6 in)

Elephant seal 4.9 m (16 ft)

Leopard seal 2.8 m (9 ft 2 in)

Life on land and sea

Seals and walruses are perfectly adapted to life in the water. But unlike other sea mammals, such as whales and dolphins, they have to give birth to their young on land.

Most kinds of seals live in groups. They may make long ocean journeys together, and then congregate on their breeding grounds, called "rookeries."

△ A colony of fur seals on rocks. Seals make their rookeries on ice or rocky islands or beaches. A rookery may contain as many as 150,000 seals.

▷ A bull (male), cow (female) and pup in a fur seal rookery. As in most species of seal, the bull is much larger than the cow. Bull seals often have several mates.

▽ A bull walrus exhibits dominant behavior, or "shows who's boss," on "haul out" grounds. Seals and walruses haul themselves out of the water onto land in large numbers for breeding or for taking a rest in the sun.

△ California sea lions fan their flippers above the water. This is done to cool down in warm weather.

◁ A gray seal under the surface. Seals close their nostrils underwater and use their tongue to close off their throat so that they do not swallow water when opening their mouth to seize prey. Seals can dive to great depths and stay underwater for long periods of time.

Seals usually breed in the spring or early summer. They haul out on rocks or shores, or on pack ice.

Cow seals come ashore only shortly before giving birth. The newborn pups are covered with a woolly "birth coat." They are suckled on their mother's milk until they can take care of themselves.

▽ A gray seal pup in its white, woolly birth coat sucks its mother's milk. It grows quickly on the rich, creamy milk.

△An elephant seal flips sand over his broad back to keep cool on the beach.

◁A sea lion plays with a diver's flipper. Most seals are friendly and trusting towards people. Yet humans are their worst enemies, killing them in their thousands for their fur.

True seals

True seals have no ear flaps. But they have perfectly good hearing.

They move very awkwardly on land because they cannot turn their hind flippers forward, and their short front flippers are more like paddles than legs. So they are reduced to a clumsy crawl on land.

It is another story in the water, where true seals are the best swimmers and divers of all the seals.

▽ A harbor seal and pup. Harbor seals are among the most common species, and are often known as common seals. They are found from Arctic waters south to the coasts of Southern California, northern Spain in Europe and South Korea in Asia.

True seals feed on a variety of fish and other seafood. Common seals eat mostly fish and octopus. Leopard seals eat fish and also penguins when they can get them. Ringed and crabeater seals feed on small shrimps.

Gray seals dive down to 100 m (330 ft) or more for flatfish and mollusks on the seabed. Elephant seals dive to deep waters for small sharks and rays.

△ A gray seal cow. Grays are large seals with mottled coloring.

▷ A common seal pup. Common seals are small and fat with round heads. They are shy creatures who haul out on isolated sandbanks and rocky ledges.

▽ A southern elephant bull and his mate. These are the largest of all seals, the bull weighing four times as much as the cow. They are called elephant seals because of the bull's trunklike nose.

▷A leopard seal surveys the scene from its ice floe. Leopard seals are solitary animals, with a reputation for being ferocious. Penguins are among their favorite foods, and they are often seen lurking in the water near a penguin colony.

They are fast swimmers, and quick over ice, too. On snow they can slither faster than a person can run. But they have never been known to attack people.

▷Leopard seals have big jaws with sawlike teeth, as even this youngster shows.

△A Weddell seal with her newborn pup. When they return to the rookery after fishing, mothers find and recognize their pups by smell.

◁Crabeater seals swimming under ice. These seals feed mainly on krill. They live around the Antarctic pack ice, and are probably the most abundant of all seals. They are hunted by killer whales and leopard seals.

Eared seals

The various types of fur seals and sea lions make up the family of eared seals. They have pointed snouts, which make them look a little like dogs. Their flippers splay out sideways when they walk.

Eared seals live in the Pacific and southern oceans. They breed in colonies. Sea lions are generally bigger than fur seals. The chief difference, however, is that fur seals have thick underfur.

▽ Galapagos sea lions on the beach. These are a type of California sea lion. They are friendly animals, and the kind most often found as performing seals in circuses.

Eared seals use all four limbs when moving on land. They swim by making long sweeps with their front flippers, "flying" through the water like penguins.

△ Eared seals use only their front flippers for swimming. The back flippers are used as rudders to change direction.

▷ A South African fur seal mother with her pup, sunning themselves on a rocky beach.

▽ Young Antarctic fur seals frisking about in the water.

△ A typical haul-out of California sea lions, draped over rocks in Monterey Bay.

◁ Steller sea lions on an Alaskan island. They breed on the coasts of the northern Pacific Ocean.

Walruses

Walruses are second only to elephant seals in size. They look like ambling, overgrown sea lions. Some experts place the two in the same family, but walruses have no ear flaps.

Although they appear clumsy and comical on land, walruses are graceful swimmers. They live only in Arctic seas and northern parts of the Pacific and Atlantic oceans. They swim south in large herds after the short Arctic summer.

▽ The walrus is a graceful animal in the water.

◁ A herd of walrus bulls on a rocky island off Alaska. Where there is not much room, walruses are quite happy to haul out onto each other, although fighting sometimes breaks out.

▽ The pink color of a sunbathing walrus contrasts with the pale color of one emerging from the water. In the sun, the blood flow to the skin increases, giving it that pink appearance.

Walruses feed on mollusks, such as clams, cockles and mussels, and other small animals found on the sea floor. They often have to dive to great depths to feed.

Light is poor on the seabed, and in winter it is completely dark in northern seas. So walruses rely mostly on touch to find their food.

Walruses dig up their prey with their snout, not their tusks as was once thought.

The story of seals and walruses

From land to water

The ancestors of seals were land mammals. Millions of years ago they adapted to life in water. Their bodies became streamlined, with the ear flap very small or absent altogether. Their four limbs developed into flippers.

The term we use for the seal and walrus group, "pinnipeds," comes from Latin words meaning feather or fin and foot. So the pinnipeds are "fin-footed" mammals.

△ Marking a gray seal pup with a colored dye. This is done to keep track of the seal population.

Hunting to live

Primitive peoples in the Arctic regions were the first to hunt seals. They ate seal meat and also used the thick layer of fat, or blubber, for oil to light the long winter nights. They used their skins to make waterproof clothing.

Many peoples depended on seals for their survival. Eskimos hunted several species of seals as well as walruses. North American Indians hunted sea lions and other species.

Hunting for profit

These and other peoples caught enough seals just for their own needs. But in the early 1700s, whalers began to kill seals for profit, mainly for their coats but also for oil, and in the case of walruses, for their tusks, too. Since then, several species have been almost exterminated.

Thanks to hunting controls imposed by some governments, the population of some species, such as the harp seal, has recovered. But other species, such as the walrus, were reduced to very low numbers in the 1700s and 1800s and have never recovered.

Human interference

The decline in the population of the three species of monk seals is due to human interference.

Sealing in the 1800s reduced the numbers of Hawaiian monk seals. Then the establishment of American naval bases in the 1940s upset their breeding, because monk seals are very sensitive to any outside intrusion.

The Mediterranean monk seal has suffered because of the loss of breeding grounds in areas that have been developed for tourism and other purposes.

Present numbers of Hawaiian and Mediterranean monk seals are estimated at fewer than 1,000 each. The Caribbean monk seal, hunted for 300 years for its oil and fur, is now thought to be extinct.

△ The Hawaiian monk seal, an endangered species.

Culling or killing

Arguments still rage over the killing of thousands of harp seal pups every year. The people who kill them cannot be called hunters, because they just club the helpless pups to death on the ice. But careful regulations have meant that the numbers of harp seals are no longer being reduced. This "culling" prevents the numbers from increasing, because the harp seal itself is responsible for reducing valuable fish stocks in the seas.

△ Performing seals in a zoo.

Seals in captivity

Performing seals have always been a favorite attraction in circuses. They are now also popular features in zoos and marine parks, or oceanariums. They are quick to learn tricks and are very agile. However, many people think that it is cruel to keep seals, or any other wild animals, in captivity.

Facts and records

Underwater feats
True seals can hold their breath for long periods of time. Weddell seals have been timed staying underwater for more than an hour without coming up for air. Eared seals, however, rarely dive for more than a few minutes at a time.

△ A young Weddell seal swimming under the ice in Antarctica.

Most abundant
The crabeater seal is the most abundant large mammal in the world. It is never possible to give an accurate estimate of the population of sea animals, but it is thought that there are at least 15 million crabeaters, possibly as many as 75 million.

△ An elephant seal bull, the largest of all the pinnipeds.

Largest
The elephant seal is the largest pinniped, bigger and heavier even than the walrus. The head to tail length of a southern elephant bull seal averages 4.9 m (16 ft) and it weighs 2.4 tons. Individual bulls have been found measuring more than 6 m (20 ft) and weighing as much as 4 tons.

Speed on ice
Most seals are slow-moving on land, especially the true seals. But the crabeater is a fast mover on ice, reaching speeds of 25 km/h (15 mph).

Glossary

Blubber
A thick layer of fat under the skin of some animals.

Bull
An adult male seal.

Cow
An adult female seal.

Culling
The reduction of a population of particular animals, sometimes in a particular place, because it is thought to be getting too big. Some seals are culled to prevent them from exhausting the stock of food fish in the seas.

Eared seals
The family of seals made up of all the fur seal and sea lion species. All have ear flaps.

Haul out
The term used when a group or herd of seals or walruses haul themselves out of the water onto land.

Krill
A kind of shrimp, found in abundance in the southern oceans, which provides a large part of the diet of some species of seals.

Mollusks
Small animals, mostly with shells, that often live on the seabed. Cockles and mussels are examples. Walruses and some species of seals feed on mollusks.

Pinnipeds
The name for the group, or order, in the animal kingdom made up of the seals and walruses.

Pup
A baby seal.

Rookery
A colony of seals or walruses where they have come together for the purpose of breeding.

Sea lion
The name given to several species of eared seals.

Species
A particular kind of animal. Animals of the same species breed young of that species.

Streamlined
Smoothly shaped for moving easily through water.

True seals
The family of seals made up of all the species without ear flaps.

Index